Practical College English

preparing for jobs & toeic

대학 실용 영어

김은경 저

기문사
www.kimoonsa.co.kr

C·o·n·t·e·n·t·s

차례

Unit 01 Do you like your new roommate?

Preview

- suggestion
- make an outline
- lose weight
- stay in shape
- for the first time
- shake hands
- instead of
- on your side
- focus on
- relate A to B
- depend on
- extend the deadline

Useful Expression

- Does she wake you up?
- Is she on a diet?
- I'm having trouble with the essay.
- It's on the second floor.
- Sometimes, people in offices and businesses work late without extra pay.
- It is not polite to ask the person's age.

Dialog 1

A : Do you have a minute?

B : Sure.

A : I'm having trouble with the essay. Do you have any suggestions about organization?

B : Yes, limit your topic and decide on your main ideas.

A : That's really helpful. What other changes do you suggest?

B : I think you should make an outline before you write your essay.

A : I certainly understand it better now. Thank you.

B : You're welcome. Come again whenever you need help. See you in class.

🕮 Dialog 2

A : Do you like your new roommate?

B : She' s crazy! she gets up at five every day.

A : Five in the morning? How come?

B : She exercises for two hours before breakfast.

A : Does she wake you up?

B : No, not a t first. She goes jogging.

A : What does she do after that?

B : She does aerobics.

A : Is she on a diet?

B : Yes, she lost 5 kilos in 1 month. I envy her.

A : Why don' t you go jogging and do aerobics with her?

B : Oh no. I' m so lazy. I can' t do it.

A : But it' s good for your health and your body.

📖 Dialog 3

A : Could I take your order now?

B : Could we have a few more minutes, please?

A : Sure. …Have you decided yet?

B : Yes. We' ve decided.

A : What will you have, ma' am?

B : I' d like an egg omelette with milk.

Daily Expression

1. 요청을 수락할 때

Q : Do you want to take a walk?

A : I' d love to.

I' d happy to.

I' d like to.

That' s sounds great.

2. 확실성을 나타내는 표현

Q : Are you able to come?

A : It' s okay with me.

Certainly.

All right.

Sure.

3. 의견을 확인할 때

Q : I've got a brand new car.

A : How do you like that?

How about that?

What do you know?

Isn't that something?

토익문법 1. 의문사로 시작하는 의문문

의문사 의문문은 질문의 첫 부분을 잘 들어야 한다. 그리고 의문사 자체는 문제를 푸는 큰 Keyword가 된다. 의문사 의문문은 Yes나 No로 답할 수 없다.

1. What

(A) what + 명사 ~ ?

ex) **What time** is the play supposed to start tonight?

→ It's printed on the brochure.

(B) what do[did] ~ ?

ex) **What do you** count as a business expense?

→ Lunch with a client, for example.

(C) what + 미래 의미

ex) **What should I do** with these tape?

→ Give them to my manager.

(D) what be(is, are) ~ ?

ex) **What is** the overseas shipping rate?

→ It depends on the distance.

실전문제

1. What color would you like the inside to be?

   a) I like that color, too.

   b) Gray, I think.

   c) No, the quality isn' t good.

2. What day did the new manager arrive?

   a) It' s the day after tomorrow.

   b) She came in yesterday.

   c) By taxi, I think.

3. What type of work do you do?

   a) Yes, it should be typed.

b) I' m currently a government surveyor.

c) We' re very pleased with your work.

4. What did the supervisor say about extending the deadline?

a) We have an extension cord.

b) She' s now happy about it.

c) Three or four feet longer.

5. What do your colleagues call you?

a) Everyone calls me Jim.

b) At the office.

c) I didn' t get a call.

American Culture - Daily life

In the United States, most people usually work from 9 a.m. to 5 p.m. People get two weeks of vacation a year. Sometimes, people in offices and businesses work late without extra pay. People also change jobs quite often. The average person will change careers – not just jobs – two or three times in a lifetime.

In the United States, most people nowadays, think regular exercise is important. They exercise at home or at a gym or health club. They play sports after school, after work and on weekends. They also bicycle, walk, swim or jog. People exercise for different reasons to lose weight, to stay in shape, or just to relax.

Unit 02 Do you like sports or what kind of recreation do you like?

Preview

- Once in a while
- prefer to
- "go dutch"
- tide up
- available
- make it
- as soon as

Useful Expression

- That sounds good.
- I' m not really familiar with the area.

- Sometimes they have name tags so you can call them by their first name.
- When people "go dutch" it means they only pay for what they ate.

🕮 Dialog 1

A : So, do you like your new home?

B : Not very much.

A : Why? It' s great! I love it!

B : I don' t like my new school.

A : Well, how do you like your new friends?

B : They' re okay, but I miss my old friends.

A : Listen, you can call them, and they can visit you.

B : Really? Can I go this weekend?

A : Yes. But you have to finish your homework first.

B : O.K. I will finish my homework today and I will visit Catherine and Amy this weekend.

A : Good girl. I hope you will like your new school soon.

B : Thanks mom. I am glad I have you.

A : It' s the first time you said like that.

🕮 Dialog 2

A : Do you like sports or what kind of recreation do you like?

B : I ski most of the time.

A : You do? Hm. That sounds good.

I' ve done a little bit myself once in a while, you know. How' d you like to go?

B : Where?

A : Oh, I don' t know. I' m not really familiar with the area.

🕮 Dialog 3

A : Where can I get some film?

B : You' ll get it at the camera corner.

A : Where is the camera corner, please?

B : It' s on the second floor.

A : What floor are we on?

B : We are on the third floor.

A : Do you have any idea where I can get fax machine?

B : Try Montgomery or K' s merchandizing.

A : May I help you?

B : Do you have film?

A : Sure. It's right here.

B : Is this on sale?

A : Yes, it's twenty percent off now.

B : Good. I'll take it.

Daily Expression

1. 일을 할 수 없는 상황

Q : Can you come here tomorrow?

A : I can't.

I can't make it.

I'm tied up.

I'm not able to.

I'm not available.

2. 초대받았을 때

Q : I'd like to invite you for dinner.

A : Thank you for inviting me.

Thank you for invitation.

Thank you for asking.

3. 곧 떠나야 할 때

Q : Oh, it's already six o'clock.

A : I have to go now.

I'd better go now.

I should go now.

I've got to go now.

토익문법 2. When

(A) 시간에 대한 간접적 대답을 하는 경우

ex) When is your department planning to hire a new supervisor?

→ As soon as they find the right person.

(B) 시간 표현이 있는 대답을 하는 경우

ex) When will the game begin?

→ In a few minutes.

→ Within an hour.

ex) When is the ship for Tokyo leaving?

→ In approximately 10 minutes.

ex) When is the payment due?

→ By the end of this week.

ex) When is the new project supposed to begin?

→ It's been put off until the spring.

Q : When did you join the Marketing Department?

A : About three years ago.

I believe it was about two years ago.

Last month.

Q : When is the project due?

A : Next Monday.

By the end of this month.

We have a few more days.

You should finish it before five o' clock today.

실전문제

1. When is your appointment with Dr. Kim?

   a) For about three months.

   b) Sometime late last year.

   c) On Tuesday afternoon.

2. When do you expect your out-of-town visitors?

   a) I visited them last January.

   b) Yes, we' re moving out of town.

   c) They should be here any minute.

3. When did the inspector approve the changes of Mrs. Chang's job?

   a) While he was here this morning.

   b) Because Mrs. Chang made several changes.

   c) Yes, he said everything was OK.

4. When will the market research study be completed?

   a) After the results are analyzed.

   b) Near the library.

   c) Yes, I've finished with it.

5. When is your appointment with the dentist?

   a) Because a filling has fallen out.

   b) Yes, I want to be a dentist.

   c) I have to be there by three.

American Culture - Video & TV Game Show

Today, there is a video store in almost every neighborhood in the United States. Nowadays, many people don't go to the movies very often. Instead they prefer to tent a video and watch it at home.

Video stores are large many types of video to rent. You can also rent videos in some supermarkets.

One of the most popular type of TV program in the United States is the game show. In most game shows, players test their knowledge on different subjects. And the questions are sometimes difficult. But there are also game shows that are games of chance. The winner must be lucky but doesn't have to be smart. There are even "dating" game shows. The prize isn't money, but a chance to meet someone new!

Unit 03 Have you ever tried golfing?

Preview

- register
- get together
- feast
- hang out
- carton
- strong urge
- overwhelmed
- cravings
- insomnia
- go away
- keep in touch
- take a vacation

Useful Expression

- I'd like to register for a TOEIC course.
- What do you do on weekends?
- Do you ever go away for the weekend?

Dialog 1

A : Excuse me. I'd like to register for a TOEIC course. Where do I go?

B : You have to go to the Foreign Language Institute, in west Hall.

A : Which one is west Hall?

B : It's gray and brown stone building just around the corner.

A : Do you know which floor it's on?

B : It's on the third floor, room 301. There's Department of English, too.

A : Thanks a lot.

🕮 Dialog 2

A : Have you ever tried golfing?

B : No. I never have.

A : What do you do in your free time?

B : Well, I really don' t have much free time.

But when I have it, I listen to music.

A : What do you do on weekends?

B : Different things. Sometimes I go shopping.

A : Do you ever go away for the weekend?

B : Yes. Sometimes I go visit my grandparents in Taejeon.

🕮 Dialog 3

A : Excuse me...

B : Can I help you, ma' am?

A : Is there a shuttle bus to downtown Vancouver?

B : Sure. Just go right through those doors.

The Airport Express stop is right outside.

A : How much is it?

B : $12.50

A : Hmm. I have a lot of baggage. How much is a taxi?

B : How many bags do you have?

A : Four.

B : How many people are there in your party?

A : Just me. I' m traveling alone.

B : Well, a taxi is around $28.00

A : OK. Thank you.

B : You' re welcome.

Daily Expression

1. 같이 만나고자 할 때

Q : We haven' t seen each other for a long time

A : Let' s get together soon

Let' s keep in touch

Let' s stay in touch

2. 다시 만나자고 할 때

Q : See you next week

A : Bye Bye

See you

Bye for now

Take it easy

Catch you later

3. 사과를 할 때

Q : I didn't tell her about it

A : I'm really sorry

I'm awfully sorry

Accept my apology

I apologize to you

토익문법 3. How

(A) How + 형용사/부사

- How many
- How much
- How long
- How soon
- How fast
- How far
- How high

ex) How high is the estimate for repainting the lobby?

→ More than two thousand dollars.

ex) How long is the warranty on this photocopier?

→ Two years including parts and labor.

ex) How long has it been since you took a vacation?

→ Over a year, so I'm ready for another.

ex) How many line workers are in this factory?

→ We have a team of about one hundred.

(B) 방법, 상태, 의견 등을 묻는 How

ex) How do I open an account?

→ You fill out this form.

(C) How about ~ ?

- How about은 What about 등과 더불어 간접적으로 권유나 초대를 하는 질문이다.

(D) 기간, 거리, 수치를 묻는 How

ex) How many cups does the man need?

ex) How many people are going to participate in the meeting?

ex) How many more desks will they need?

ex) mow much longer will they wait?

(E) 빈도를 묻는 How

ex) How often the man work out?

ex) How many times a year did the woman used to fly to Japan?

[빈도표현]

- Every three months = Every quarter(quarter 1/4 분기)
- Twice a week
- Three times a week
- Once a month

(F) 수단

ex) How will the woman travel?

ex) How will the men get to the airport?

ex) How will the document be delivered?

실전문제

1. How much did the property sell for?

   a) Twice its original value.

   b) Yes, you did it properly.

   c) Right next to the bank.

2. How long have you been in your present apartment?

   a) Thank you very much.

b) For nearly two years.

c) That's about right.

3. How many workers do they intend to transfer?

a) Yes, I plan to leave tomorrow.

b) Three hundred people will be relocated.

c) He's worked there for several years.

4. How many mechanics work on the day shift?

a) Three Shifts a day.

b) There are usually eleven of them.

c) From eight until five thirty.

5. How have you arranged to get to the conference?

a) Yes, quite a range.

b) I'm getting a ride with a colleague.

c) To the south of the capital city.

American Culture - Thanksgiving

On the fourth Thursday in November, in houses around the United States, families get together for a feast or a large meal. almost all families eat turkey and cranberry sauce for this meal and have pumpkin pie for dessert. This feast is part of a very special day, the holiday of Thanksgiving. Thanksgiving is a day on which we celebrate and give thanks.

Unit 04 I'd like to mail this package to New York.

Preview

- make eye contact
- emphasis on
- vacancy
- customs and Immigration
- direction
- destination
- venue
- itnerary
- take over
- maternity leave

Useful Expression

- I'd like to mail this package to New York.
- How would you like to send it?
- I have a lot of trouble with pronunciation.
- I'm calling about your ad for a job vacancy.
- I didn't quite catch your name.
- I'm not on the phone.
- How long will it take?
- you should make eye contact with the Customs and Immigration officers.

Dialog 1

A : I'd like to mail this package to New York.

B : How would you like to send it?

A : First class, please.

B : OK. Let's see. It's ten pounds, so that'll be twelve dollars and sixty-one cents.

A : How long will it take?

B : About two days.

A : Thank you.

Dialog 2

A : Where are you studying English?

B : I' m a student at the institute.

A : Really? I study there, too. I like the classes very much.

B : I have a lot of trouble with pronunciation.

A : Pronunciation isn' t very difficult for me. The grammar gives me trouble.

B : Don' t put too much emphasis on grammar. For me, I never understand when the teacher speaks fast.

A : I had trouble with that at first. I understand better now.

Dialog 3

A : Are you ready to order?

B : Yes, we are.

A : Good. What would you like this evening?

B : I' ll have the spaghetti with meatballs.

A : And what would you like, sir?

C : I' d like a steak, medium-rare, please.

A : would you like soup or salad with that?

C : Soup, please.

Daily Expression

1. 상대방의 생각에 찬성할 때

Q : He'll help you today.

A : That sounds good.

That's a good idea.

That's sounds great.

What a good idea!

I'd appreciate that.

2. 근심 걱정을 표현할 때

Q : Are you ready for your job interview?

A : I'm nervous about it.

I'm worried about it.

I'm anxious about it.

3. 칭찬할 때

Q : How do you like her cooking?

A : It's very good.

Well done.

She does a fine job.

It's excellent.

Good job.

토익문법 4. Who

■문장 구조 유형

(A) Who + will + 동사원형

ex) Who will take over Mrs. Simpson's position when she goes on maternity leave?

(B) Who + be + ~ing

ex) Who's traveling with you?

→ I'll be on my own this time.

(C) Who + be + 명사

ex) Who was the last person to use the copy machine?

(D) Who + 동사

ex) Who made this spicy noodle dish?

■Who에 대한 대답 유형 3가지 분석

ex) Who is in charge of delivering the packages to the office?

1. Sandy usually handles it.
2. My assistant. Ms, Smith.
3. I don't know exactly.

실전문제

1. Who took this photograph?

a) My friend did.

b) With a god camera.

c) Last weekend.

2. Who's going to take Ms. Lee to the airport?

a) To catch a plane.

b) About twenty minutes.

c) Robert can do it.

3. Who do you think will be selected to lead the committee?

a) I think it's too small to read.

b) It'll probably be Mr. Proctor.

c) That sounds like a good choice.

American Culture - Eye Contact

When you are at Customs and Immigration, you should make eye contact with the Customs and Immigration officers. Because Americans usually look directly into the eyes of people they are talking with.

If you don't keep eye contact with the Customs officers he or she might think you are not telling the truth or you may not be listening or you are not polite.

Unit 05

Would you show me your boarding pass?

Preview

- boarding pass
- assignment
- be supposed to
- turn out
- wait for
- leave for
- domestic flight
- depart from
- inaugurate
- make a mistake
- confirm your reservation
- charge for
- make a reservation

Useful Expression

- May I help you find your seat?
- How did it turn out?
- What have you got in your hand?
- Only cars with 3 people or more can drive in these commuter lanes.

Dialog 1

A : Would you show me your boarding pass?

B : Here it is.

A : May I help you find your seat?

B : Yes, please. It's 25A.

A : Follow me, please. Your seat is right here by the window.

B : Thank you.

🕮 Dialog 2

A : Hey, Susan. Did you get good notes from the lecture today?

B : Well, pretty good, I think.

A : We have to finish the history assignment by Wednesday, right?

B : Yeah, by Wednesday. We're supposed to read another chapter from the textbook, aren't we?

A : What pages did you write down?

B : I wrote pages 161 to 178.

🕮 Dialog 3

A : Good morning, Mr. Kim. How are you, today?

B : Just fine, thank you. Is Mr. Brown in?

A : Yes, he is. Mr. Brown is expecting you. Please take a seat and wait a second.

A : Oh, Mr. Han. How are you?

B : Fine, thank you, and you, Miss Lee?

A : I'm fine, too. Do you want to see Mr. Brown?

B : Yes, please.

A : I'm sorry, but Mr. Brown is in a meeting right now.

B : That's OK. I just dropped to say hello.

Daily Expression

1. 용서해 줄 때

Q : I broke your sun glasses.

A : That' s all right.

Don' t worry about it.

These things happen.

We all make mistake.

We' re all human.

2. 실수

Q : Who did it this?

A : I made a mistake.

It' s all my fault.

3. 좋지 않은 소식을 들었을 때

Q : My father is in the hospital.

A : That' s too bad.

That' s terrible.

That' s a shame.

What a shame.

I' m sorry to hear that.

토익문법 5. Where

(A) 주어와 관련된 장소를 묻는 Where

1. Where + be + 주어
2. Where + 조동사 + 동사원형
3. Where + be + 주어 + going to

(B) 목적어와 관련된 장소를 묻는 Where

Where 뒤의 주어보다는 동사 + 목적어 그 중에서도 목적어가 무엇인지 파악한다.

실전문제

1. Where's the best place to get office furniture?
   a) A sunny location would look nice.
   b) The store on the corner has a good selection.
   c) Chairs, tables, desks, and lamps.

2. Where is John's new apartment?
   a) Because the rent is low.
   b) Very close to his office.
   c) With an extra bedroom.

3. Where are the theater tickets?

a) Thanks. I'm looking forward to it.

b) At eight o'clock in the evening.

c) I have them in my pocket.

4. Where will Ms. Hamasaki sit at the awards luncheon?

a) We're expecting sixty guests.

b) Shortly after lunch.

c) At the head table.

5. Where did David leave the invitations?

a) In the mailboxes.

b) Before the discussion.

c) No, he didn't.

American Culture - Hotel

When you reserve a hotel room in the United States, you may have to give your credit card number to confirm your reservation. Then, if you change your mind at the last minute and don't show up, you may still be charged for the room. But it is not always necessary to make a reservation for a room. You can just walk into any hotel and ask for a room.

In the United Stated, a double room in a hotel usually has one large queen-size or king-size bed. If you need a room with two beds, you should ask for a twin room. Almost all of the rooms have private bathrooms with a shower over the bathtub. However, in the U.K. you are given a choice of facilities like a single room with a shared bathroom, a single room with a private bathroom or a single room with a private shower.

Unit 06 May I take your order?

Preview

- available for
- appetizer
- cuts in the line
- care for
- make line
- make sure
- connected to
- take your order
- care for
- rely on
- count on

Useful Expression

- Do you have any rooms available for tomorrow night?
- What are your rates?
- May I take your order?
- What side dish would you like with that?
- Would you care for some dessert?
- I'd like to get some information on New Zealand.
- Have you ever been there?
- Are you in line?
- Is this the line for tickets?

Dialog 1

A : Good morning, Marriott Hotel. Can I help you?

B : Yes, please. Do you have any rooms available for tomorrow night?

A : Yes, we do. Would you like a single or a double?

B : A double, please.

A : And for how many nights are you staying?

B : For three nights, please.

A : Fine.

B : What are your rates?

A : It's $85 per night. Could I have your name, please?

B : Oh, yes. Sure. It's Mike.

🕮 Dialog 2

A : May I take your order?

B : Yes, please. For the appetizer I'd like the fruit cocktail.

A : And what kind of salad would you like?

B : I'll have the spinach salad.

A : And for the main course?

B : I'd like the prime rib, please.

A : What side dish would you like with that?

B : Um, I think I'll have mixed vegetables.

A : Would you care for some dessert?

B : Yes, I'll have an ice cream sundae.

🕮 Dialog 3

A : Good evening, ma' am.

B : Good evening. I want to check in.

A : Do you have a reservation?

B : Yes, I do.

A : What name?

B : E.K Kim.

A : Just a moment... I don' t have your name on the computer.

B : Try my company. That' s Samsung Marketing

A : Ah, yes. I have it here. Samsung Marketing, 1276 Market street, San Diago. Ms. Kim. A single room for five nights.

B : That' s right.

A : And the room' s reserved on your Visa card?

B : Yes, It is.

Daily Expression

1. 좋은 소식을 들었을 때

Q : I got a teaching job at the school.

A : That' s wonderful.

That' s fantastic.

I'm very happy to hear that.

I'm very happy for you.

2. 적당한 말이 생각나지 않을 때

Q : Can I work with him?

A : Well, let's see.

Let me see.

I don't know what to say.

I don't know.

3. 약속

Q : I promise to be there on time.

A : Can I count on you?

Can I depend on you?

Can I rely on you?

토익문법 6. Which

(A) Which + 명사

ex) Which side of the street do they drive on in China?

→ The opposite of here.

→ The same side as they do here.

→ On the right side.

ex) Which desk is yours?

→ The one on the left.

(B) 의문사 Which

1. Which is ~ ?
2. Which of you ~ ?

실전문제

1. Which man is the Director of Cultural Affairs?

a) The one in gray.

b) A formal affair.

c) From different countries.

2. Which of you approved this loan application?

a) I can lend you some.

b) John okayed it.

c) It was hard to prove.

3. Which is the faster route to your house, the new highway or North Avenue?

a) They must be lost.

b) The highway is quicker.

c) Yes, we'll be at home.

American Culture - Are You In Line?

Americans usually make lines when there are more than two people waiting for the same service. If someone "cuts" in the line, people get angry at that person. If you want to get some service you should stand in a line and make sure that it is the line that you want to be in. You can ask "Are you in line?" or "Is this the line for tickets?"

If you are the first person to make a line, you should be behind the yellow line.

Unit 07

How was the trip?

Preview

- look for
- density
- on the rocks
- interested in
- apply for
- take out a loan
- do my best
- appreciate

Useful Expression

- Could you come up with Hong Kong's well-known high-rises?
- How was the trip?
- I had a very interesting traveling companion.
- What would you like to drink, sir?
- When a job opening is advertised there are often a lot of people interested in applying.

Dialog 1

A : Look at those blinking lights around that highest building.

B : That's Central Plaza, which is the highest of all the high-rise buildings in Hong Kong.

A : Really? I understand that Empire State Building in New York is a 102-story high-rise. Which is the higher of the two?

B : Of course, Central Plaza doesn't compare to Empire State Building. It has 78 floors.

A : Could you come up with Hong Kong's well-known high-rises?

B : Well, 70-story Bank of China Tower, 65-story Howell

Centre, 53-story Sun Hung Kai Centre, 52-story Jardine Centre, and Exchange Square --- just to name a few.

A : That many in this city of high density?

🕮 Dialog 2

A : How was the trip?

B : Really great! I had a very interesting traveling companion.

A : Oh, I know what that means. Tell me about her.

B : She was about twenty four or twenty-five. She had big brown eyes. She was very friendly. I' m sure she' s a open-minded person.

🕮 Dialog 3

A : I see you are a chain smoker.

B : You' re right.

A : How many packs a day?

B : Half a carton a day.

A : As many as five packs a day?

B : Yes. It' s quite a hassle to resist the strong urge to smoke.

Daily Expression

1. 소식을 전할 때

Q : How did you know that news?

A : I' ve heard.

People say.

They told me.

Everyone says.

2. 가능성이 있는 상황

Q : It looks like it' s going to rain soon.

A : May be.

You never know.

There is a chance.

It' s a possibility.

3. 날씨

Q : How is the weather in Korea?

A : It' s raining.

It' s wet.

It' s soggy.

Is' s damp

토익문법 7. 선택의문문

질문유형

A. Would you like your coffee now, or would you rather wait?

B. Are you buying the car with cash, or are you taking out a loan?

C. Do you like the green stripes, or the blue?

선택의문문의 answer 유형

A. both – either – neither

- Actually, neither
- It makes no difference.
- Neither, it's ~ .
- Both sound good.
- Either one is fine. / Either will be fine.
- Actually, I like both.

ex) Would it be preferable to call in the afternoon or evening?

→ It doesn't normally make a difference.

B. 모르겠습니다

- I don't know.
- I have no idea about that.
- Not that I know of.
- I've not decided yet.

- Whichever you prefer.
- I' m not sure.

C. 상관없어요

- It doesn' t matter.
- I don' t care.

D. ~에 달려있지요.

- It depends on ~

ex) Did you like jazz or classical?

→ It depends on my mood.

실전문제

1. Will the delivery department lease or purchase its new vans?

   a) We can deliver the vans.

   b) It' s included in the purchase price.

   c) They' ll lease them for now.

2. Would you prefer a single or a double room?

   a) I' m not hungry.

   b) No, I don' t.

   c) Either is fine.

3. Do you want us to start this project now, or leave it for tomorrow?

   a) I'll do my best.

   b) It can wait until the morning.

   c) No, I don't want it, thanks.

4. Would you like a lift, or will you walk?

   a) It's OK, it didn't fall.

   b) I'd appreciate a ride.

   c) I thought it would work.

5. Are you looking for a domestic cheese or an imported one?

   a) One that was made locally.

   b) She's from Germany.

   c) Yes, extremely important.

American Culture - Job Interview

When a job opening is advertised there are often a lot of people interested in applying. Many job hunters send in their resumes and apply for the same position. The job interview, therefore, is very important. In the interview, an applicant must demonstrate that he or she is the best person for the job.

For example, successful applicants dress appropriately and have a clean and neat appearance. They go to the interview alone and are always on time.

At the beginning of interview, the applicant shakes hands firmly with the employer. During the interview, it is appropriate to smile often and look directly into the eyes of the interviewer.

The applicant is prepared to answer questions about education and previous jobs. They ask questions about the applicant's personal background, family and hobbies. Interviewers expect applicants to talk proudly, confidently, and truthfully about their work experience, skills, goals and abilities.

When the interview is over, the applicant stands up, shakes hands with the interviewer and says thank you.

Job applicants who can show they are capable, well prepared, polite, and honest have a better chance of getting the job they're looking for.

Unit 08 Have you been to the United States?

Preview

- personnel
- majored in
- get off
- position
- in charge of
- prescription
- warranty
- requisition
- belong to

Useful Expression

- Do you have any special skills?
- What position do you hold?
- I'm in charge of the downtown San Francisco area.
- How long have you been with Samsung?

Dialog 1

A : Miss Lee, please come in. I'm Mike Kim. Director of personnel.

B : I'm pleased to meet you.

A : So, you want to be a secretary at S.K Company. Tell me about yourself, please.

B : Well, I'm 20 years old. I majored in computer networking at Chungkang college.

A : Do you have any special skills?

B : Yes, I can use computers very well.

A : If you enter this company, what department would you like to work in?

📖 Dialog 2

A : Excuse me. Does this train go to lnsa-dong?

B : No, it doesn' t.

You have to take this train to Chongno 3-ga, and then transfer to the orange line, and then...

A : Wait. I' m sorry. Where do I transfer?

B : At Chongno 3-ga station.

A : Chongno 3-ga station, and then which train do I take?

B : Take the orange line, the line three.

And get off at An-guk station.

If you get our of the ground, you can find the entrance to Insa-dong way.

A : OK. The orange line.

How many stops is it from Chongno 3-ga?

B : Hmmmm. ... just one stop.

Dialog 3

A : Have you been to the United States?

B : Yes. I just visited my relatives living in Los Angeles. I' m looking forward to the summer, when I can visit them again for a week.

A : What' s the purpose of your visit?

B : I' m thinking about studying overseas at the graduate level. As far as I know, American education offers a rich field of choices for international students.

A : There is such a wide variety of educational institutions, programs and locations that the choices may overwhelm international students.

Daily Expression

1. 일기예보에서 쓰는 표현

※ 온도 : It' s warm.

It' s hot.

It' s chilly.

It' s nippy.

It' s cold.

It' s freezing.

※ 날씨 : Thunder shower.

Isolated rain.

Drizzling.

Pouring.

Cat' s and dogs.

heavy rain.

It is rain.	is	– 100% 현재 된 상태
It must be rain.	must be	– 90% 정도의 가능성
It may be rain.	may be	– 70% 정도의 가능성
It might be rain.	might be	– 50% 정도의 가능성
It could be rain.	could be	– 30% 정도의 가능성
It is not rain.	is not	– 0% 않은(없는)상태

※ 예를 들어 어떤 상태나 그 정도를 예측.

He always goes there.	always	– 100%
He usually goes there.	usually	– 90%
He often goes there.	often	– 70%
He sometimes goes there.	sometimes	– 50%
He seldom goes there.	seldom	– 20%
He rarely goes there.	rarely	– 10%
He never goes there.	never	– 0%

※ 일상 하는 버릇의 정도.

토익문법 8. 일반의문문

1. Do, Did로 시작하는 의문문

(A) 현재형 Do 의문문

ex) Does the warranty include parts and labor?

→ Yes, but it doesn't cover upgrades.

ex) Does it rain a lot in that part of the country?

→ Not at this time of year.

(B) Do you know + who/when/why ~ ?

ex) Do you know why Raymond left the Seoul firm?

→ He took a job Busan.

ex) Do you know when it's supposed to stop raining?

→ No, I haven't heard.

ex) Do you know anyone who works in the design department?

→ Not a soul.

ex) Do you know when they're leaving for Manila?

→ At ten tomorrow.

(C) 과거형 Did 의문문

ex) Did you place the requisitions in their appropriate folders?

→ Yes, I put them in the filing cabinet.

실전문제

1. Does the second shift end soon?

   a) In two more hours.

   b) No, in the middle.

   c) Move it to the left.

2. Do you think we'll close early tomorrow?

   a) That clock has the right time.

   b) Not as long as it seems.

   c) Yes, we can all leave at three.

3. Doesn't the bookstore stay open late tonight?

   a) Yes, a good selection of magazines.

   b) I was late this morning, too.

   c) No, they close at five.

4. Do you know who these documents belong to?

   a) I'll try not to take too long with them.

   b) No, I can't find anything.

   c) They must be George's. He was here earlier.

5. Didn't you study engineering?

   a) Yes, mechanical engineering.

   b) Because he likes it.

   c) A new motor.

American Culture - Health

In the United States, most people only go to a doctor when they are sick. They usually spend about ten minutes with the doctor. The doctor can usually say what the problem is very quickly and often give them prescriptions for some medicine. The prescriptions can be filled at drugstores. If not, the doctor may suggest to them to go to a specialist.

People with colds and coughs don't susually go to a doctor but to a drugstore to buy some medicine. In a drug store, people buy over-the-counter drugs for colds, coughs, sore throats and other common illnesses.

유용한 실용영어 회화 표현

1. Here you go again.
   또 시작이군.

2. Snap out of it.
   꿈깨.

3. Don't make a fuse.
   수다 떨지 마라.

4. I'm stuck speechless.
   기가막혀 말이 안나온다.

5. You are as quiet as a mouse.
   쥐 죽은 듯이 조용하다.

6. That's a rip off!
   바가지 쓰셨군요.

7. That's a steal!
   공짜나 다름없군요!

8. I'm worried sick.
   걱정 돼 죽겠다.

9. I did well on my test.
   시험 잘 봤어요.

10. for an age
    오랫동안

11. I'd like to make withdraw.
(은행에서) 돈을 찾으려고 한다.

12. How would you like that?
저거 어때?

13. Old habits die hard.
세 살 버릇 여든 간다.

14. That's money down the drain.
그건 돈 낭비다.

15. I'm sorry to hear that.
그거 안됐군.

16. He will get back on his feet in no time.
그는 곧 일어 날 거야.

17. It's out of the question.
말 도 안돼.

18. My car stalled.
차가 고장이 나서 섰다.

19. Your gonna have to junk it.
그 차를 폐기처분했다.

20. They cooked up a scheme.
그들이 계략을 꾸몄다.

21. Here you go again.
또 시작이군.

22. I know a thing or two.
나는 조금 안다.

23. What's wrong?
무슨 일이니?

24. Let me take a look at it.
어디보자

25. We can't afford it.
그것 살 수 없다.

26. Have you lost weight?
너 살빠졌니?

27. It wouldn't hurt to go look?
가서 보는 것 정도야 괜찮겠지?

28. I'd look great behind the wheel.
운전하는 내 모습은 멋져 보일거야.

29. It's a token of my appreciation.
작은 성의이다.

30. You got what you pay for.
비싸면 비싼대로 좋다. 싼게 비지떡이다.

31. You name it, you get it.
말만 하세요, 다 있습니다.

32. I'd like give it a try.
내가 한번 해볼께.

33. Fools rush in.
서둘러서 좋을 건 없다.

34. I want a rush service.
빠른 서비스를 원한다.

35. A.S.A.P.(=As soon as possible)
가능한 한 빨리

36. D.U.I.(driving under influence)
음주운전

37. Where are you calling from?
어디 전화하는 거니?

38. He is dying to see you.
그는 네가 보고싶어 죽을 지경이다.

39. Something came up.
무슨 일이 생겼어.

40. Don't count your chickens before they are hatched.
김치국 마시지 마라.

41. What kind of business are you in?
무슨 일 하세요?

42. What's gotten into her?
저 여자 왜 저래?

43. You still have feeling for him.
너는 여전히 그를 좋아한다.

44. I pulled my muscles on my back.
허리를 삐끗했다.

45. He is making a big deal out of it.
별거 아닌거 가지고 수선떤다.

46. While you are at it, could you refill my coffee?
이왕하는 김에 커피를 더 주세요.

47. You always stick up for him.
항상 그의 편만 든다.

48. The pie is on the house.
파이는 서비스입니다.

49. Get out of face.
꺼져.

50. Let' s drink night away.
밤새도록 한잔하자.

51. I' m manging in there.
그럭저럭 지낸다.

52. Drop me a line.
편지 좀 하세요.

53. Spill it.
비밀을 다 털어 놓다.

54. So, sue me!
그래 어쩔래!

55. I get up with the chickens.
새벽에 일찍 일어나다.

56 Jump the gun.
서둘러 결론을 내리다.

57. Poor thing!
불쌍해라!

58. You look familiar.
얼굴이 낯익다.

59. I think you've got the wrong person.
사람을 잘못 보신 것 같군요.

60. Can I try this on?
이것 입어봐도 됩니까?

61. How does it fit?
사이즈가 잘 맞나요?

62. The boss makes a face at me.
사장이 나에게 인상을 썼다.

63. I break up with her. =I'm through with her.
그녀와 깨졌다.

64. I'm looking for a tie to go well with this shirt.
이 셔츠에 어울릴 넥타이를 찾고 있습니다.

65. I'll ring it up for you.
계산하겠다.

66. Is this on sale?
세일하는 것입니까?

67. It's 30 percent off.
30% 세일이다.

68. The price was recently marked down.
가격이 인하되었습니다.

69. How much do I owe you?
얼마입니까?

70. That's a good buy(good deal, real bargain)!
싸게 사셨군요.

71. That's a steal.
공짜나 다름없군요.

72. That's a rip off!
바가지 쓰셨군요.

73. I'm 3 dollar's short.
3달러 부족합니다.

74. alumni meeting
동창회

75. We have a lot in common.
우린 공통점이 많아.

76. arrianged marriage
중매 결혼

77. I'd like to open an account.
계좌를 개설하고 싶어요.

78. bankbook
통장

79. I heard it through the grape vine.
소문을 통해 들었다.

80. Just leave it there.
그냥 놔 두세요.

81. I'm all thumb.
잘못해요.

82. I'm out of shape.
몸매가 엉망이예요.

83. I went on a fool's errand.
헛걸음했다.

84. You're just like I thought you'd be.
내가 생각한 대로 군요.

85. Get off me.
저리 비켜.

86. Some parents you are!
대단한 부모군요.

87. You're getting off the subject.
주제에서 벗어난 얘기를 하고 있어요.

88. I'm all for it.
동감이야.

89. Would you move over a little?
조금만 비켜 주시겠어요?

90. This is a small gift from me.
약소하지만 받아주시겠어요?

91. How brave of you!
배짱도 좋다.

92. Let's put it a vote.
표결에 붙입시다.

93. You're not making sense.
말이 앞뒤가 안맞는다.

94. maternal side/paternal side
외가/친가

95. I don't get it.

이해가 안돼.

96. I have mixed feeling./It's bitter sweet.

시원 섭섭하다.

97. You pinhead!

이 돌머리야.

98. Look who's talking.

사돈 남말하네.

99. It can't be helped.

어쩔 수 없었어.

100. I'm gonna go for it?

내가 해 볼께?

101. You look great dressed up.

차려 입으니 멋지군요.

102. paper, scissors, rock

가위, 바위, 보

103. You're making a scene here.

다들 너를 처다보고 있어.

104. What a windfall!

왠 떡이야.

105. Enjoy your meal.

맛있게 드세요.

106. It makes my mouth water.

This food makes me drool.

이 음식이 군침돌 게 하는 군요.

107. No pain, no gain.

고생끝에 낙이 온다.

108. come to think of it.

가만히 생각해 보니,

109. I'm just browsing.

I'm just looking around.

그냥 구경만 합니다.

110. Cash or charge?

현금인가요, 카드인가요?

111. Take your time.

천천히 하십시오.

112. It's up to you.

당신에게 달려 있습니다.

113. So far so good.

지금까지는 좋습니다.

114. Drop me off at this store.

이 가게에서 내려주세요.

115. I can't think of it off hand.

금방 생각이 떠오르지 않네요.

116. It's a pain in the neck.

정말 지겨운 일이네요.

117. It's up to my ears in work.
일이 산더미 처럼 쌓여있어요.

118. The cokes are on me.
콜라는 내가 사겠어요.

119. That's a close call.
큰일 날뻔 했어요.

120. My chances are slim.
가망이 없어요.

121. You name it.
말 만하세요.

122. Not on your life.
어림없는 소리

123. I'll keep my fingers crossed.
행운을 빌겠어요.

124. He's gone for the day.
그는 퇴근 했어요.

125. After you, please.
먼저 하세요.

126. We are in the same boat.
같은 처지군요.

127. What a small world!
참 좁은 세상이군요.

128. It doesn't make any difference to me.
제겐 아무거나 상관없어요.

129. It's not myself today.
오늘 제정신이 아니군요.

130. Let's get to the point.
본론으로 들어갑시다.

131. Who's in charge?
책임자가 누구입니까?

132. Don't get me wrong.
나를 오해 하지 마세요.

133. If I were in your shoes
당신 입장이라면

134. Are you pulling my leg?
날 놀리시는 겁니까?

135. Three more hours to go.
세 시간이 더 남았다.

136. Neck and Neck
막상막하

137. It's Greek to me.
무슨 뜻인지 모르겠습니다.

138. Stick around.
기다려 봐요.

139. Take you pick.
하나 골라 보세요.

140. Things are looking up.
점점 나아지고 있어요.

141. Not bad for an amateur.
아마추어치고는 괜찮은데.

142. I ache all over.
온 몸이 쑤신다.

143. I'm returning your call.
제게 전화하셨다면서요.

144. What's the best time for you?
When is convenient time for you?
언제가 가장 좋으세요?

145. Let's meet halfway.
조금씩 서로 양보합시다.

146. We'll have to wait and see.
두고 봐야 합니다.

147. He had it coming.
혼날 만한 짓을 했군요.

148. All is well that ends well.
끝이 좋아야 다 좋다.

149. We made it.
해냈다.

150. Couldn't it cause side effects?
부작용은 없을까요?

151. He's driving me up the wall.
그 남자 때문에 미치겠어요.

152. I don't touch the liquor.

나는 술안마신다.

153. I'm social drinker.

분위기에 맞추어서 한잔한다.

154. How about a drink after work?

근무 끝나고 한 잔 어때?

155. You up for it?

그러고 싶은 마음이 드니?

156. You twisted my arms.

네가 억지로 시켰다.

157. We don't have money to burn.

우리는 낭비할 돈이 없다.

158. I did well to marry her.

그녀와 결혼하길 잘했다.

159. Quit singing you own praises.

자랑 좀 그만해라.

160. I gave him a talking-to.

그에게 한소리 했다.

161. in a dog's age

오랫 동안

162. Mr.(Miss) right.

이상형

163. I hear you.

동감이야.

164. That's a good point.
바로 그거야.

165. You've learned to pay lip service.
아부할 줄도 아는 군요.

166. I hear you lound and clear.
정말 그래요.

167. He's a little edgy.
그는 신경이 날카로워요.

168. I have to cram for the finals.
나는 기말시험 벼락공부해야 되.

169. The price is out of line.
너무 비싸요.

170. The night's still young.
아직 초저녁이다.

171. I locked out of my room.
열쇄를 방 안에 두고 나왔다.

172. It made a good impression on me.
그것은 나에게 좋은 인상을 주었다.

173. It's a hot item.
그건 아주 잘 팔 리는 제품입니다.

174. It's settled.
자 그럼 결정됐다.

175. If my memory serves me right
제 기억이 맞는다면

176. My mouth is watering.
군침도는 군요.

177. I'll buy the second round.
두 번째 잔은 내가 살게요.

178. It really works.
정말 효과가 있었어요.

179. How was it?
어땠어요?

180. First come, first served.
선착순

181. I can't pinpoint it.
그런 건 아냐.

유용한 표현

1. Not that I'm aware of. = I don't know.

2. I'm not sure.

3 It hasn't been decided yet.

4. What do you think of your new position?

5. How do you like your new job?

6. He is not qualified for the position.

7. She's not right for the position.

8. The numbers just don't add up.

9. You have to fill out this form. = You have to fill in this form.

10. You should have prior approval.

11. She's meeting a client downtown.

12. How much did it cost to run the newspaper ad(vertisement)?

13. He's going to drop off his resume.

14. How long have you worked here?

15. The company covers your health expenses.

16. We have many distribution channels.

17. Productivity is up by ten percent this quarter.

18. We've documented everything.

19. The apartment is still vacant. = The apartment is still unoccupied.

20. Do you have a key to the dressing room?

21. I'm taking a shortcut.

22. It took me three hours to get there.

23. It's located in the suburbs of Seoul.

24. It's too soon to tell.

25. We're open from nine to six.

26. Spring is just around the corner.

27. Are you in a hurry to go somewhere?

28. There's no hurry.

29. Does anyone have a spare stapler around here?

30. She is expecting in about a month.

31. It's already been taken care of.

32. I'll get right on it.

33. Do you have time to go to the movies this Friday?

34. Are you free this Friday?

35. That would be great. = That's a good idea.

36. Where are you heading for? = Where are you headed for?

37. We are heading over to the office.

38. I'm looking forward to meeting you again.

39. He was satisfied with the result.

40. He was dissatisfied.

41. The store closed down.

42. I'll check with him later.

43. I just turned twenty nine.

44. At 9:00 o'clock sharp.

45. Why didn't I think of that!

46. You should have brought your concerns to my attention earlier.

47. I really need a job. Is the paper the best place to look for work?

48. I can make it by 7:30 if I hurry.

49. She won't be here until Thursday.

50. All the houses I liked were out of my price range.

토익 문법 총정리

1. 부사

- 접속 부사

however	moreover
therefore	nevertheless
furthermore	thus

ex) I gave a presentation. However, the audience didn't like it.

ex) We met the sales target. Therefore, we got the incentive.

- 시간의 부사

already yet still

ex) The meeting has already started.

ex) I haven't received the letter yet.

ex) Have you read the letter yet?

ex) We are still expecting a pay raise.

- 부정의 부사

seldom hardly rarely

ex) He seldom says no to his boss.

실전문제

1. The chairman hasn't signed the contract (already / yet).

2. Their office supplies are good. (However / Furthermore), they are cheap.

3. They (seldom / not) have problems with the product.

4. We were short of money. (Nevertheless / Moreover), we decided to develop a new product.

2. 수동태

be interested in	be supposed to
be covered with	be faced with
be filled with	be confused wit
be satisfied with	be accustomed to
be pleased with	be involved in
be dedicated to	be related to

be devoted to　　　　　　　　　　be committed to

ex) The customers are not satisfied with the quality of the product.

ex) The management seems to be pleased with the outcomes.

실전문제

1. We are faced (with / of/ in) some economic difficulties.

2. They are dedicated (at / to / with) developing a new program.

3. This matter is not related (about / of / to) his mistake.

4. This matter is not related (about / of / to) his mistake.

5. The agency was interested (at / in / with) hiring more consultants.

6. The conference room is filled (of / with / in) newly hired employees.

A. The new employee is not accustomed __________ working with lots of people

a) about b) to c) with d) in

B. We are committed providing high-quality service to our customers.

a) to b) with c) in d) of

3. 수동태 + to 동사원형

be asked to	be required to
be allowed to	be advised to
be scheduled to	be invited to
be forced to	be expected to
be told to	be intended to
be supposed to	be encouraged to

ex) They were forced to leave the company.

ex) You are not allowed to use the computer.

ex) They were told to attend the seminar.

ex) The event is scheduled to take place next month.

실전문제

1. Participants __________ make hotel reservations themselves.

2. The event __________ start in an hour.

3. The sales representatives __________ arrive soon.

4. The president __________ be here.

4. 특별 용법

1) 부정대명사 some과 any

1. some과 any는 단독으로 쓰일 수도 있고, 다른 일반 명사와 함께 쓰일 수도 있다.

Some people complained about overtime work. (some+명사)

There were 100 people in the gathering. Some didn't enjoy it very much. (some=some people)

2. some과 any는 셀 수 있는 명사, 셀 수 없는 명사와 함께 쓸 수 있다.

Some candidates were not present at the campaign event.

I need some advice from you.

You cannot use any services without my permission.

3. some은 주로 긍정문에서, any는 부정문, 의문문, 조건문에서 쓰인다.

I have some questions to ask you.

I don't have any questions.

If you have any problems, let me know.

5. 명사의 특별 용법

1) 항상 복수형으로만 쓰이는 명사

바지, 안경 가위 등과 같이 원래 두 개의 짝으로 이루어진 물건들은 항상 복수형으로 쓴다. 이 명사들은 항상 복수 취급하고 복수 동사를 쓴다.

glasses pants scissors jeans

2) 맨 뒤에 -s가 붙어서 복수형으로 착각하기 쉬운 명사

학명(economics 등)을 나타내는 명사들은 s가 붙지만 단수 명사로 단수 동사를 쓴다.

economics , mathematics , linguistics news

3) 단수형과 복수형이 같은 명사

다음 명사는 단수형과 복수형이 같다.

a means – a lot of means

a species – many species

a series – three series

4) 가산이냐 불가산이냐에 따라 의미가 달라지는 명사

셀 수 있는 명사로 쓰였을 때	셀 수 없는 명사로 쓰였을 때
a room	enough room
many times	time
a fire	fire

6. 형용사의 특별 용법

※ 혼동하기 쉬운 형용사

considerable	considerate
successful	successive
terrible	terrific
favorite	favorable
awful	awesome

※ 토익에 자주 출제되는 형용사 표현

be aware of	be likely to
be eligible of	be ready to
be able to	be responsible for
be capable of	be subject to

7. 부사의 특별 용법

접속 부사

접속 부사는 두 개의 문장을 의미상 자연스럽게 연결하는 역할을 한다. 접속 부사는 주로 이어지는 문장의 바로 앞에 위치하거나 문장의 중간에 위치한다.

접속 부사의 종류		
however	moreover	therefore
nevertheless	furthermore	thus

I gave a presentation. However, the audience didn' t like it.

We met the sales target. Therefore, we got the incentive.

시간의 부사

already	yet	still

The meeting has already started.

I haven' t received the letter yet.

Have you read the letter yet?

We are still expecting a pay raise.

부정의 부사

부정의 의미를 포함하고 있으므로 not이나 never와 같은 부정어와 함께 쓰일 수 없다.

seldom	hardly	rarely

He seldom says no to his boss.

다음 괄호 안에서 알맞은 것을 고르시오.

1. The chairman hasn't signed the contract (already / yet).
2. Their office supplies are good. (However / Furthermore), they are cheap.
3. They (seldom / not) have problems with the product.
4. We were short of money. (Nevertheless / Moreover), we decided to develop a new product.

8. 시제 일치 특별 용법

주장, 요청, 제안, 충고를 나타내는 문장에서의 시제 일치의 예외

주어	insist recommend demand suggest advise request	that	주어	(should)	동사원형

The doctor suggested that he quit smoking for his health.

They requested that the guests refrain from making any noise.

She insisted that Mike make a presentation this time.

다음 괄호 안에서 알맞은 것을 고르시오.

1. The manager suggested that we (hired/hire) more secretaries.
2. My boss demanded that we (worked/ work) even on weekends.
3. The accountant recommended that I (uses/use) the new accounting program.
4. I advised that he (quits/quit) compiaining about his boss.

9. to부정사의 특별 용법

to부정사를 취하는 동사

want to V	refuse to V	wish to V	manage to V
hope to V	propose to V	offer to V	ask to V
plan to V	expect to V	need to V	decide to V
fail to V	afford to V	agree to V	promise to V

to부정사를 취하는 명사

ability to V	plan to V	time to V	chance/oppo rtunity to V
right to V	effort to V	way to V	decision to V

to부정사를 취하는 형용사

be able to V	be willing to V	be pleased to V	be easy/ difficult to V
be eager to V	be likely to V	be about to V	be ready to V

5형식 문장에서 목적격 보어로서의 to부정사와 원형부정사

• to 부정사를 목적격 보어로 갖는 동사

want, would like, advise, allow, encourage, force, ask, order, tell, invite, require, expect	+목적어+목적격보어(to부정사)

Mr. Han is expecting me to attend the seminar.

They asked him to wait outside.

• 원형부정사(동사원형)를 목적격보어로 갖는 동사

사역동사와 지각동사는 5형식 구조에서 원형부정사를 목적격보어로 갖는다.

I had the mechanic fix my car. (사역동사)

My coworker helped me (to) finish the report. (준사역동사)

I saw Jim talk with his boss yesterday. (지각동사)

10. 동명사를 목적어로 갖는 동사

반드시 동명사를 목적어로 취하는 동사

이 동사들 다음에 동사를 쓸 때는 반드시 [동사원형+ing]형태로 써야 한다.

enjoy	deny	practice	postpone
mind	avoid	suggest	recommend
consider	risk	admit	give up
finish	keep	miss	put off

They are considering renovating the cafeteria.

Do you mind working on the weekends?

James suggested getting new office furniture.

자주 쓰이는 동명사 표현

have difficulty V-ing	cannot help V-ing
be busy V-ing	look forward to V-ing
spend (time/money)V-ing	be good at V-ing
there is no use V-ing	be devoted to V-ing
be worth V-ing	be used to V-ing
feel like V-ing	be accustomed to V-ing

I had difficulty finding a firm to work at.

We look forward to working with you.

He is not accustomed to using a smartphone.

11. 부가의문문

(A) 본 문장(동사: 긍정) + 부정 부가의문문

ex) You' ve been to London before, haven' t you?

→ Have you been to London before?

(B) 본 문장(동사: 부정) + 긍정 부가의문문

ex) You haven' t been to London before, have you?

→ Yes, I have (= I have been to London before.)

ex) You don' t have any money I can borrow, do you?

→ Sure, how much would you like?

실전문제

1. You didn' t happen to see my umbrella anywhere, did you?
   a) No, it didn' t happen that way.
   b) Yes, you left it in the cloakroom.
   c) Red and blue.

2. Raj said he would measure the width of the stage, didn' t he?
   a) I believe it' s made of wood.
   b) The show is two hours long.
   c) Yes, he' ll be here this afternoon.

3. This graph shows an interesting trend, doesn' t it?
   a) No, at eleven o' clock.
   b) Yes, it certainly does.
   c) The shows are all sold out.

4. It's starting to get really dark out, isn't it?

a) They're predicting a storm.

b) No, I didn't start yet.

c) We could paint it white.

5. You said there would be a ten percent discount, didn't you?

a) Not more than twenty or thirty people.

b) I haven't counted them up yet.

c) That only applies to large orders.

6. The gardeners have been doing a good job, haven't they?

a) Yes, the grounds look great.

b) I'm not looking for a job.

c) Several kinds of flowers.

7. You filled out a claim form, didn't you?

a) No, do you think it's necessary?

b) Yes, it was already full.

c) Did he claim it was?

8. The new line of women's sportswear has been quite successful. hasn't it?

a) No, the line isn't straight.

b) Yes, I play tennis twice a week.

c) Yes, sales are unexpectedly high.

9. Jake Williams' book about management strategies is excellent, don't you agree?

a) He missed the strategy meeting.

b) I just started reading it last night.

c) Yes, the agreement was signed.

10. We sent them an invoice, didn't we?

a) Yes, two weeks ago.

b) He's a bookkeeper.

c) No, it's not too loud.

11. You're going to Dr. Hall's retirement party, aren't you?

a) Yes, but I'll be a little late.

b) A table for six, please.

c) When I retired a few years ago.

12. It seems like managers are getting younger, doesn't it?

a) We were all very hungry.

b) No, they didn't manage to finish.

c) Yes, Mr. Kang is only twenty-eight.

12. 평서문

실전문제

1. The oven isn't working properly.
   a) No, you're right, I haven't.
   b) Thanks, I'm glad you like it.
   c) But it was checked only yesterday.

2. I'm surprised that Jim Cooper made such a competitive offer.
   a) He really wants that contract.
   b) We watched the game on television.
   c) Yes, I can help you.

3. Our customers have requested that we stock a wider range of greeting cards.
   a) Has anyone seen her?
   b) That's a good idea.
   c) He's very agreeable.

4. This kind of construction produces much better results.
   a) But it's more expensive.

b) She's very kind.

c) Yes, these are the instructions.

5. I've been shopping at this store for years.

a) No, I don't hear any.

b) It's on Forest Avenue.

c) We appreciate your business.

6. We've decided on a sports theme for the company picnic.

a) No, she's on the other team.

b) I can never make up my mind.

c) Great! That sound fun.

7. We really need to update the telephone directory.

a) Yes, the staff has changed a lot.

b) You can use my phone.

c) No, I didn't leave a message.

8. I'm waiting to see Professor Abraham.

a) He'll be with you in just a moment.

b) Let me know when he's ready.

c) If that's all right with you.

9. The bottle on the water cooler needs to be changed again.

a) No, thanks. I'm not thirsty.

b) I don't have any change.

c) That's the third time this morning.

10. Our accountant wants you to contact her in reference to last month's revenue statement.

a) By telephone, usually.

b) June, July, and August.

c) I'll return her call after lunch.

토익 중요 어휘정리

1. 비즈니스 관련

shipping company
construction company
law firm
accounting firm
department
accounting department
personnel department
human resources department
sales department
public relations(PR) department
marketing department
payroll department
engineering department
department store
division
section
conference = meeting
convention
conference room = meeting room
boardroom
minutes
supply
demand
stock market
invoice
proposal
order
sign a contract
inventory
take an inventory of
cover
office supplies
copier = photocopier = copy machine = Xerox machine
photocopy
stapler
paper clip job interview
resume
cover letter = covering letter
position

apply for
applicant
candidate
freelance
payday
catalog
accounting
bookkeeping
bookkeeper
supplier
courier
bike messenger
clerk
desk clerk = receptionist
homemade
domestic
session
training session
orientation
briefcase
briefing
bankrupt
bankruptcy
go bankrupt

2. 직업, 신분 관련

carpenter
clerk
customer
colleague
travel agent
nutritionist
counselor
waitress
loan officer
teller
athlete
insurance agent
mechanic
motorist
nurse
real estate agent
aerobic instructor

3. 전화 관련

extension (number)	telephone operator
I'm calling to	I'm calling about
regular customer	coupon
status	inconvenience
free of charge	place an order
process	state
apologize	return one's (phone) call

He's not here right now. = He's not in at the moment. = He's out right now. = He stepped out.

The manager just stepped out for lunch.

He'll be back soon. = He'll be back in a moment.

He'll be back this Friday.

Would you like to leave a message? = Could I take a message?

Hello, you've reached ~

This is Bart Simpson from G&C Corporation.

I'm returning your call about the order you placed last week.

We apologize for any inconveniences we may have caused you.

Please give me a call as soon as possible.

I really appreciate your help.

Please leave your name and mailing address to receive an invitation to our grand reopening.

📖 Dialog

A : Could you please tell me when Dr. Kates is available today?

B : He has an opening at 4:30. Do you want me to schedule you for that time?

A : Sure. I don't see any problem with that.

4. 컴퓨터 관련

motherboard	monitor = screen
printer	scanner
modem	adapter
plug-in	software
hardware	hardware store
hard drive	spreadsheet
word processing	password
encrypt = encode	function
install	log onto the internet
outdated = out-of-date	

The computer program doesn't function properly.

The motherboard has the capacity to install the printer, but you need an adaptor for the plug-in.

5. 기계, 기구, 자동차 관련

projector	overhead projector
apparatus	equipment
device	cell(ular) phone = mobile phone
vending machine	appliance
dishwasher	refrigerator = fridge
refrigerate	dryer
vacuum cleaner	(water) purifier
loudspeaker	lawnmower
furnace	paintbrush
tool room	technician
carpenter	maintenance
valve	headlight
microscope	eyepiece
test tube	magnifying tool
crack	operate
repair = fix	combine
overheat	keep ~ rolling
make an audio-visual presentation	
be equipped with	break down

This plant is equipped with the high-tech machinery.
Why don't you call her on her cell phone?
Everything seems to be in good working order.

Next time you bring it in, we'll do a tune up.
The car broke down.

6. 식당, 요리 관련

cook	chef
banquet	bill
split a bill	order
recipe	appetizer
dessert	(calm) chowder
shrimp	garlic
pasta	dairy product
blade	dull
sharp	call for
turn down	chop
special	dish
steak	seafood
shellfish	poultry
pork chops	lamb chops
herb	herbal
blend	complement
water cooler	cutlery
veggie	dairy (product)
delicious	full-bodied
fruity	hearty

spicy
lean
health conscious

Can I take an order, sir?
I think you've overcharged me for my meal.
She dined with Mr. Lee in the Italian restaurant.
After the lunch rush passes.
The blade is too dull.

7. 예약 관련

make a reservation
book
reserve
confirm
confirmation

I've booked a table for five at Bario's tonight.
We're fully booked for the 27th.
You're booked on a Monday morning light out of Tokyo.
I booked a flight to New York.
I'd like to reserve a van for three days.

8. 병원 관련

surgeon
physician
dentist
clinic
ward
maternity ward

medication	chart
medical exam(ination)	(medical) checkup
first-aid	emergency surgery
make an appointment	palpitation
heart palpitation	numb
numbness	symptom
flu	ailment
allergy	an allergy to pollen
be allergic to	sneeze
stomach ache	stomach flu
emergency room = E.R	nursing home
pharmacy	pharmacist
medical history	prescribe
prescription	fill one's prescription
prescribed drug	over-the-counter drug

I don't have the symptoms today.
I'm on medication.

9. 여가, 여행, 공연, 티켓 관련

a season ticket	refund
box office = ticket office	ticket window
ticket holder	performance
play	tour operator

souvenir
backpack
suitcase
resort
driving range
pole
slope
camp out
(tour) guide
itinerary
landmark
monument
senior trip
tent
sleeping bag
7th grader
sightsee
sightseeing
arrive
arrival
cancel
cancellation
pack
stretch
await = wait for
adhere to
look forward to
scenic
initial
approximately = about
hopefully

Tickets were all sold out.
They rave about the new play.
It was overrated.
It's a steal.

10. 일기예보, 교통정보 관련

– 일기예보

weather forecast
precipitation

blizzard

tornado

hurricane

high-pressure band

The chances of rain is 70 percent.
Winds are light and from the east at ten miles per hour.
There is a strong high-pressure band across the entire region.
We are expecting quite a bit of rain for your weekend.
We'll have more on that in the next half-hour.

- 교통정보

public transportation

intersection

gas station

arrival time

cab = taxi

on foot

board

be on board

give ~ a ride = give ~ a lift

commuter

rush hour

ramp

icy

multi-vehicle pile-up

vantage point

freezing

monitor

He gave me a ride. = He offered me a ride.
The airport bus drivers are on strike and the line-up for taxis were very long.
Mechanical problems delayed our flight.
I just missed the twelve o'clock train by ten minutes.
The next train to Osaka isn't until 3p.m.

Traffic was backed up for miles because of a six-car collision on the freeway.

I'm glad we reserved a car with bunks.

Let's walk down to the dining car for a drink.

There is a multi-vehicle pile-up on Alberta Drive and traffic is backed up for about a mile.

11. 점검, 검열 관련

annual	annually
inspection	inspect
safety check	battery
smoke alarm	smoke detector
go off	mock fire drill
regulation	observe
observance	observation

12. 업무, 사무실 관련

office supply store	stationery store
business card	item
merchandise	brochure
branch	reception desk
probationary period	dress code
attire	agent
agency	warehouse

plant	auto plant
storage	inventory
occupation = profession = vocation	CEO = chief executive officer
director	secretary
coordinator	supervisor
contractor	counselor
assignment	delivery
work order	work late
work overtime	take over for
relieve	be on leave
board meeting	seminar
session	budget
proposal	management
price quote	discount
expense	travel expenses
projection	partnership
assess	assessment
profits	margin
loss	shortage
invest	investment
manufacture	manufacturer
bureau	confidential
incentive	encourage
attain	exceed
hire	promote

productive
productivity
input
output
quarter
quarterly
purchase
cut back on
curtail
eliminate
terminate
arrange
renew
renewal
contract
renew the contract
contract renewal
meet
meet the customer' s needs
meet budget goals
real estate developer
realtor
property
landlord
premises
(law)suit
file
client
clientele
attorney = lawyer
tax regulator
balance
account
loan
teller
exchange rate
cash
paycheck
lay off = fire
layoff
payroll
justify
retire
retirement
benefit
retirement benefits
benefit from

The company cut the number on payroll. = The company laid off some employees.

He was fired.

How can they justify the layoff with the profits the make?

He was promoted to senior manager.

He didn't get a promotion

They want to cash their paychecks.

How long have you been (working) with MTC?

We've been working on the project for over a month.

Should we discuss the contract over breakfast/coffee?

This company is suffering from soaring costs.

Our projects always go over budget.

We should consider doing some hiring.

I can't stand this new manager.

He wants the employees performance to improve.

You're expected in advertising at 11:00.

My meeting will likely go past 5:00.

Do you know how much time we're allotted to speak at the conference?

13. 비행기 및 공항 관련

– 기내방송

flight	boarding pass
pilot	flight attendant = stewardess
tray table	cabin
cockpit	cruising height

frequency

layover = stopover

destination

immigration

immigration official

entry form

nationality

customs declaration card

customs officials

duty

duty-free items

traveler' s check

take off

conflict

ascend

descend

exceed

upright

prior to

make sure (that)

just a reminder

Your attention, please.

We would like to remind everyone that mobile phones, note books, and CD players must be turned off in the cabin.

This is because the frequencies of these portable appliances may conflict with operational equipment in the cockpit.

Please be advised that tray tables and seat backs should be in their full upright position until we have completed take off.

In about half an hour we will be landing in Bangkok.

Upon arrival, a customs declaration card must be properly filled out and submitted to customs officials.

You must inform them of all items you are taking in to the country.

If you have exceeded the $500 limit, you will have to pay duty on those items.

Our layover will be just one hour.

– 비행기 연착, 취소 관련

shutdown	maintenance
accommodation	lodging
arrangement	entrance
voucher	inclement
complementary	be advised to
result from	

Attention passengers for Air Canada 797 to Toronto.

Due to inclement weather and thunderstorm warnings, Flight 797 has been canceled.

14. 광고

clearance (sale)	seasonal (sale)
grand opening	specialty
ornament	decoration
draw	receipt
promotion	featured item
representative	sales representative

feature	incorporated = Inc.
limited = Ltd.	remainder
panel	rating
odor	stench
landfill	treatment
upholstery	gallon
recycle	reuse
donation	donator
donate	reasonable
compact	cost effective
ever-increasing	statewide
incredible	foul
musky	hypoallergenic
dedicated to	give away
commemorate	point out
erase	fit into
stand in for	stand-in
launch	woo
estimate	currently

We are pleased to present our after-Christmas sale.

You will find savings of up to 30% on all items.

YDR is celebrating its thirty-year anniversary this March with special events in all of its locations all month long.

Prize draws will be held every day between 12 and 4.

I'm here to tell you about our newest product.
This product has some incredible features that they won't be able to do without.

15. 정리세일

slow sales
fittings
go out of business
close down
mark down
permanently
Everything must go!

Due to slow sales, it has no choice but to close its doors forever.
All stock is discounted, with power tools marked down a quarter and bathroom fittings discounted by up to forty percent.
Everything else is reduced to half price for quick clearance.

16. 세미나, 워크숍, 컨벤션 소개

barrier
language barrier
communications barrier
mediation
mediate
psychologist
psychology
therapy
headquarters
headquarters office
effective
effectively
improve communications between
bring in

feel free to	brainstorm
come up with	transition
a new arrival	guideline
community activities	profession = occupation = vocation
function	settle in
time management	efficient
efficiency	voluntary
volunteer	urge
benefit from	convention
participant	keynote speaker
closing address	closing speech
entitled	annual
workshop	presenter
attendee	senior (citizen)
fitness	the public
for–profit organization	nonprofit organization
exhibit	exhibition
venue	pass
rear	hallway
doorway	setting
accessory	biking = cycling
introductory	innovative
administrative	planetary
frightening	continuously
focus on	approach

strive
strive for

attend to
vote on

kick off

Please feel free to brainstorm to come up with new ideas.

We brought in three new members.

She has over ten years experience helping new arrivals and it isher responsibility to ensure that your transition is as smooth as possible.

Mr. Jackson is a time management specialist and is going to be speaking about how to maximize efficiency in all aspects of your life.

You can attend a whole host of seminars ranging from A to B.

Our keynote speaker, Dr. Johnson, will give our closing speech Saturday night entitled, "?IT Industry in Asia."?

There will be shows open to the public all weekend from non until 9:00 p.m.

17. 연사, 게스트 소개

authority
researcher

foundation
anthropology

anthropological
anthropologist

charity
alumni

fundraising event
daycare center = child care center

artifact
reminiscence

practice

security

internet service provider

emergency meeting

landscaping company

ferry

take part in = participate in

preserve

groundbreaking

recognized

indigenous

passionately

implication

security system

operation

congress

rain forest

conduct a study on

get started

preservation

vigorous

doctoral

passionate

devoted to

Today, we're pleased to have Dr. George Black with us.

Today, we're pleased to have with us Dr. George Black, senior researcher at the Cielo Institute.

He will be taking questions from the audience later in the program.

18. 공사

renovation

plan

panel

crew

damage

completion

air purifier

tenant

vandalism	ergonomics
ergonomic	leaking
extensive	intensive
minimum	maximum
minimize	maximize
apply	consult
report to work	enhance
offer	be in the process of
be in progress	in an effort to
coupled with	due to
sparingly	

> We are currently in the process of upgrading all our facilities.
> The work will be in progress from May 6th until June 2nd.

19. 회의

executive	management
notice	branch
downsizing	R&D = Research and Development
emergency	gain
reward	procedure
adjourn	replace
replacement	apply
summon	summons

substitute
represent
absent
absence
unexpected
year-end
short handed
temporary
temporarily
at the last minute
on one's behalf

Thank you for coming to this meeting on such short notice.

We are short handed at the moment with many staff away on business.

I've been asked to take on his responsibilities until he returns next week.

That is why I have summoned all of you.

Sales in the last quarter have increased by as much as 20%.

In order to appropriately reward everyone here, we will be offeringa year-end bonus of 10% to all current employees.

20. 경제 뉴스

merger
merge
acquisition
M&A = Merger & Acquisition
stock
bond
shareholder
labor dispute
tariff
import tariff
backup tape
domestic
domestic sales
domestic market

secondary
duty-free
evaluate
assess
expand
decline
flow
long-standing
implement
evaluation
assessment
expansion
ensure
provide A with B = provide B for(to) A

21. 시상식

achievement
sponsor
scholarship
principal
proceeding
corporate
excel
labor of love
sponsorship
varsity
administrator
corporation
outstanding
on behalf of

22. 박물관

sculpture
modernist
depart
be off to
feature
impressionist
wing
departure
explore

It's my pleasure to welcome you to the National Art Museum. Before we head out, I want to quickly run through our schedule of activities.

First, we'll have a chance to see the Picasso Exhibit, featuring many of his most famous works.

23. 기타

aisle	aisle seat
window seat	award ceremony
wedding reception	invitation
take place	suit
casual clothes	dress casual
dress formally	warehouse
electricity bill	warranty
lease	license
garage	mechanic
repair	broom
dustpan	package
book shelf	parking lot
booth	newsstand
generator	confusion
sign up for = enroll in = register for	registration
describe	description
eat out	go on a trip

go on a picnic

come by = drop by = stop by

subscription

contain

translation

check over

check out

turn off

spare

external

urgent

inappropriate = improper

costly

talkative

unfortunately

janitor

custodian

floorboard

patio

big box store

rug

blazer (coat)

workout

the press

editor

run into

subscribe to

accommodate

translate

hand in = submit

check in

turn on

on time

brand new

internal

appropriate = proper

suitable

uneventful

fortunately

nanny

dress shirt

valuables

jewelry

fountain

lounge

complex

complex

leather

stable

generate

editorial	generator
oil spill	remainder
refund	celebrate
replace	anniversary
rejection	return
replacement	defect
defective	bachelor' s degree
master' s degree	Ph. D. = doctor' s degree
doctoral	doctoral thesis
dissertation	coauthor
psychology	psychologist
botany	botanist
borrow	deal with
undertake	load A with B
find out	run out
run out of	go over = review
stop by = drop by = come by	negotiate
inform A of B	supplement
review	sympathize
extend	screen
accompany	demolish
destroy	make do with
drop off	refuse
notify A of B	remind A of B
ought to = should	anticipate

splurge on

spill

make it

what if ~ ?

tedious = tiresome

temporarily

currently

designated

proper

as well

immediately

afterwards

alongside

moonlight

fulfill

be of assistance

unacceptable

temporary

current

shortly

deplorable

properly

in advance

mistakenly = by mistake

on top of

중요 어휘와 표현

1. be supposed to 동사

ex) I' m supposed to see my dentist today.

ex) You are not supposed to park here, sir.

ex) It is supposed to rain today.

2. pick up

ex) He picked his friends up at 6:00 p.m.

ex) I picked up some cheese and eggs.

ex) Who is going to the garage to pick up the car?

3. mind

ex) Do you mind if I smoke here?

→ Actually, I do mind.

→ Not at all. = No problem.

4. build in / built-in / built-in furniture / come with

ex) Does the computer come with a modem?

→ Sure, it' s built in.

ex) It comes with a warranty.

5. bring up = raise

ex) You were brought up around here, weren' t you?

→ Yes, I was born and raised here.

6. be eligible for / **benefits / put in = spend**

ex) When is the last order due to be shipped?

→ Not until you' ve put in one year' s service.

7. ship / shipment

ex) When is the last order due to be shipped?

→ We expect it will leave tomorrow.

8. bill = check

ex) When were we billed for the renovations on the third floor?

→ We received the invoice two weeks ago.

9. bid / deadline

ex) By when do we have to have our bid submitted?

→ Five o' clock is the deadline.

10. business expense

ex) What do you count as a business expense?

→ Lunch with a client, for example.

11. outside line

ex) How do you get an outside line from this phone?

→ Just press 9 and dial the number.

12. car pool / car pool lane / rush hour

ex) Do you use the car pool lane during rush hour?

13. figure out

ex) We don' t know but we' re trying to figure it out.

14. combination (lock) / combination

ex) I always forget the combination.

15. sort

ex) Everything is sorted by date.

16. a second helping

ex) I' ll have a second helping.

17. have a hard time ~ing = have difficulty (in) ~ing = have trouble ~ing

ex) I had some difficulty with the work.

ex) I had difficulty (in) doing the business with Mr. Wang.

ex) I had difficulty with the restrictions you placed on the project.

18. place an order / fill an order / in stock / out of stock

ex) We can't fill their order for 300 bottles of beer, because we have only 200 currently in stock.

ex) We're out of stock.

ex) The part is not in stock.

19. schedule / reschedule

ex) The seminar is scheduled for 2:00 p.m.

ex) When is she scheduled to arrive?

ex) I'd like to reschedule it for Friday morning at 10:00 a.m.

20. bid / subdivision

ex) Kinglish Construction is gong to submit a bid for that new subdivision.

21. lease / condominium / efficiency (apartment)

ex) I just singed the lease for a condominium on Denver Street.

22. pass away = die / pass out = faint

ex) My grandfather passed away.

23. get a hold of

ex) I'm trying to get a hold of Mr. Robert.

24. turnout

ex) There was a large turnout at the conference.

25. first thing

ex) I'll do it first thing in the morning.

26. come along

ex) How is your new assignment coming along?

27. staple

ex) Please staple your receipt to the form.

28. hold off from ~ing

ex) I'll hold off from purchasing a van.

29. misconduct

ex) He was reported for misconduct.

30. in front of

according to

across from

in spite of

in addition to

regardless of

31. regarding

    including – excluding

    concerning

32. due to, owing to.

토익 기출 표현

1. sort through papers
2. call from a public phone
3. feed the birds by the water
4. the bottles stacked on top of each other
5. fix the roof
6. examine a product
7. a car door left open
8. a large flower arrangement on the table
9. work at the construction[building] site
10. the woman exercising on indoor track
11. the conductor leading the group
12. people helping themselves to food
13. take a photogragh
14. people waiting to board the train
15. crops planted in rows on the hillside
16. heavy machinery at the construction site
17. wear suits and ties
18. hold one's bag on the shoulder.
19. go around in a circle

20. play a game outdoors

21. push a cart

22. point to a document

23. work at the keyboard

24. the housed build in the similar style

25. sweep the path

26. go down the steps

27. the man drinking from his glass

28. the musician performing outside

29. work on the electrical cables in the area

30. the men plying cards

31. standing room only on the street car

32. the trees lost most of their leaves.

33. the audience facing the front of the room

34. the boat tied up off the shore

35. make a selection from the menu

36. the bicycles having baskets in the front

37. use the laboratory equipment

38. the couple strolling arm in arm

39. pay for one's purchase

40. hold a stack of cleaning towels

41.talk to each other

42. make copies

43. boats running under the bridge

44. work on the wires[electrical cables]

45. cross the street

46. rest on the porch

47. look in the baskets

48. have a break in a staff lounge

49. a man wearing glasses

50. stand with one's arms crossed

51. feed the goat

52. decorated cakes

53. have their picture taken

54. examine the documents

55. equipment laid out on the counter

56. work in the green house

57. throw the ball into the air

58. select books from the selves

59. smile at the customer

60. move a load of dirt

61. the water flowing over the rocks

62. many windows along the side of the barn

63. reach for an item on the shelf

64. exchange their business cards

65. bend over the drinking fountain

66. look at a telephone directory
67. dig the ground
68. wrap up the food in the foil
69. throw away the paper plate
70. dip their toes in the pond
71. cross the finish line
72. rest her chin in her hand
73. look through a microscope
74. button her jacket
75. play the string instruments
76. look over the railing
77. post a notice on the bulletin board
78. the barber trimming the customer's hair
79. fill the car with fuel
80. improve the roadway
81. the man making a speech
82. hold some papers in her hand
83. the man standing close to the edge of platform
84. the women walking beside the river
85. operating fountains
86. wear a large hat
87. look at some architectural plan
88. receive an award

89. the plane landed a short while ago

90. the desks arranged near the wall

91. pick up some pieces of wood

92. the musicians playing outside

93. the men fishing on the shore

94. stand in line

95. work at the drafting table

96. the roof in need of repair

97. get the food ready to be served

98. record the presentation

99. the people taking a rest on the rock

100. share the office space

101. roll up the blueprint

102. pour some coffee for the man

103. the people lined up to board the train

104. lean on a crutch

105. arrange the chairs in a row

106. hold a test tube in her hand

107. the construction equipment pouring concrete

108. examine a light bulb

109. adjust the sound system

110. address to the public

111. the doctor examining the patient's foot

112. light up the candles

113. piles of plates on the table

114. bushes planted along the path

115. the man sitting behind the wheel

116. the truck backing out of the garage

117. vacuum the carpet

118. sunbathe on the beach

119. the patient getting an injection

120. the woman resting on the steps

121. the man taking his dong for a walk

122. the man brushing leaves off the car

123. enjoy themselves at the party.

124. the hall decorated with balloons

125. cash register on the table

126. the hallway crowded with people waiting

127. knit on the chair

128. the cables running several directions

129. wear glasses and lab coats

130. carry a bucket

131. stand on the ladder

132. shovels leaning against the fence

133. the dentist attending a patient

134. completely bare landscape

135. waitress taking an order

136. sweep up the leaves

137. weigh some produce

138. sip a cup of coffee

139. fold up the chair

140. pull on a glove

141. have a handbag on the lap

142. place baked goods on display

143. the presenter using a projector

144. be about to hit the ball

145. the vehicle elevated for repairs

146. trail going through the woods

147. work on a roof

148. the cabins overlooking the lake

149. the woman having her temperature taken

150. the railing running in front of the benches

151. play a musical instrument

152. passengers boarding the train

153. shake hands each other

154. interview taking place outdoors

155. point something on a page

156. hand out some pamphlets

157. fly a kite

158. be surrounded by the potted plants

159. chop up the vegetables

160. play a sport

161, pull over to the side of the road

162. use a fishing rod and line

163. sit at a control panel

164. salute the flag

165. a lot of boxes in the warehouse

166. bright and spacious lobby

167.greet each other with a handshake

168. the woman focusing her camera

169. the bicycles pulled behind the car

170. the building under construction

171.care for the flower bed

172. look at the items in the display case

173. the man wearing a striped shirt

174. the couple walking past the police officer

175. sketch a work of art

176. dispose of some litter

177. pile luggage on a cart

178. the shelves filled with various kinds of pots

179. rolls of paper lined up on the floor

180. direct traffic

181. people fishing at the water's edge

182. the man working at a drawing table

183. the road passing through a forest

184. the chairs piled up beside the pool

185. the pedestrian heading toward the archway

186. point to an image

187. stand to make a point

188. sing together

189. the woman wearing a backpack

190. have dressed formally

191. work at the sewing machine

192. houses on one side of the street

193. the child sitting on a swing

194. crates full of fruits

195. close the lid of waste basket

196. people gathered in a circle

197. the building overlooking the water

198. the carton boxes being loaded into the car

199. wrap a package

200. use a wheelbarrow

유용한 표현

1. Not that I'm aware of. = I don't know.

2. I'm not sure.

3 It hasn't been decided yet.

4. What do you think of your new position?

5. How do you like your new job?

6. He is not qualified for the position.

7. She's not right for the position.

8. The numbers just don't add up.

9. Youhave to fill out this form. = You have to fill in this form.

10. You should have prior approval.

11. She s meeting a client downtown.

12. How much did it cost to run the newspaper ad (vertisement)?

13. He's going to drop off his resume.

14. How long have you worked here?

15. The company covers your health expenses.

16. We have many distribution channels.

17. Productivity is up by ten percent this quarter.

18. We've documented everything.

19. The apartment is still vacant. = The apartment is still unoccupied.

20. Do you have a key to the dressing room?

21. I'm taking a shortcut.

22. It took me three hours to get there.

23. It's located in the suburbs of Seoul.

24. It's too soon to tell.

25. We're open fromnine to six.

26. Spring is just around the corner.

27. Are you in a hurry to go somewhere?

28. There's no hurry.

29. Does anyone have a spare stapler around here?

30. She is expecting in about a month.

31. It's already been taken care of.

32. I'll get right on it.

33. Do you have time to go to the movies this Friday?

34. Are you free this Friday?

35. That would be great. = That's a good idea.

36. Where are you heading for? = Where are you headed for?

37. We are heading over to the office.

38. I'm looking forward to meeting you again.

39. He was satisfied with the result.

40. He was dissatisfied.

41. The store closed down.

42. I'll check with him later.

43. I just turned twenty nine.

44. At 9:00 o'clock sharp.

*저|자|소|개

■김 은 경

- 이화여자대학교 영어영문학과 졸업
- 럿거스 뉴저지 주립대(Rutgers NJ State University) 사회학 석사
- 럿거스 뉴저지 주립대학 사회학 박사과정 수료
- 고려대학교 강사
- 캘리포니아 대학교 산타크르즈(University of California, Santa Cruz) 테솔
- 동국대학교영어교육학 박사

현) 청강문화산업대학교 관광영어과 교수

Practical College English(대학실용영어)

●발행일

2012년 8월 20일 초 판 인쇄
2012년 8월 31일 초 판 발행

●저 자

김 은 경

●발행인

한 인 환

●발행처

도서출판 **기 문 사**
서울시 동대문구 용두2동 730-4번지 홍신빌딩 3층
전 화 : 02) 2265-7214, 922-8662~3
팩시밀리 : 02) 922-8772
homepage : www.kimoonsa.co.kr
e-mail : book@kimoonsa.co.kr
등 록 : 1978. 8. 9. NO. 6-0637
ISBN : 978-89-7723-553-3 93740

정가 : 10,000원